My Recipes

....

Contents

Recipe Nº. 1 ....

Recipe Nº. 2 ....

Recipe Nº. 3 ....

Recipe Nº. 4 ....

Recipe Nº. 5 ....

Recipe Nº. 6 ....

Recipe Nº. 7 ....

Recipe Nº. 8 ....

Recipe Nº. 9 ....

Recipe Nº. 10 ....

Recipe Nº. 11 ....

Recipe Nº. 12 ....

Recipe Nº. 13 ....

Recipe Nº. 14 ....

Recipe Nº. 15 ....

Recipe Nº. 16 ....

Recipe Nº. 17 ....

Recipe Nº. 18 ....

Recipe Nº. 19 ....

Recipe Nº. 20 ....

Recipe Nº. 21 ....

Recipe Nº. 22 ....

Recipe Nº. 23 ....

Recipe Nº. 24 ....

Recipe Nº. 25 ....

Recipe Nº. 26 ....

Recipe Nº. 27 ....

Recipe Nº. 28 ....

Recipe Nº. 29 ....

Recipe Nº. 30 ....

Recipe Nº. 31 ....

Recipe Nº. 32 ....

Recipe Nº. 33 ....

Recipe Nº. 34 ....

Recipe Nº. 35 ....

Recipe Nº. 36 ....

Recipe Nº. 37 ....

Recipe Nº. 38 ....

Recipe Nº. 39 ....

Recipe Nº. 40 ....

Recipe Nº. 41 ....

Recipe Nº. 42 ....

Recipe Nº. 43 ....

Recipe Nº. 44 ....

Recipe Nº. 45 ....

Recipe Nº. 46 ....

Recipe Nº. 47 ....

Recipe Nº. 48 ....

Recipe Nº. 49 ....

Recipe Nº. 50 ....

Recipe Nº. 51 ....

Recipe Nº. 52 ....

Recipe Nº. 53 ....

Recipe Nº. 54 ....

Recipe Nº. 55 ....

Recipe Nº. 56 ....

Recipe Nº. 57 ....

Recipe Nº. 58 ....

Recipe Nº. 59 ....

Recipe Nº. 60 ....

Recipe N°. 61 ....

Recipe N°. 62 ....

Recipe N°. 63 ....

Recipe N°. 64 ....

Recipe N°. 65 ....

Recipe N°. 66 ....

Recipe N°. 67 ....

Recipe N°. 68 ....

Recipe N°. 69 ....

Recipe N°. 70 ....

Recipe N°. 71 ....

Recipe N°. 72 ....

Recipe N°. 73 ....

Recipe N°. 74 ....

Recipe N°. 75 ....

Recipe N°. 76 ....

Recipe N°. 77 ....

Recipe N°. 78 ....

Recipe N°. 79 ....

Recipe N°. 80 ....

Recipe N°. 81 ....

Recipe N°. 82 ....

Recipe N°. 83 ....

Recipe N°. 84 ....

Recipe N°. 85 ....

Recipe N°. 86 ....

Recipe N°. 87 ....

Recipe N°. 88 ....

Recipe N°. 89 ....

Recipe N°. 90 ....

Recipe N°. 91 ....

Recipe Nº. 92 ....

Recipe Nº. 93 ....

Recipe Nº. 94 ....

Recipe Nº. 95 ....

Recipe Nº. 96 ....

Recipe Nº. 97 ....

Recipe Nº. 98 ....

Recipe Nº. 99 ....

Recipe Nº. 100 ....

Recipe Nº. 101 ....

Recipe Nº. 102 ....

Recipe Nº. 103 ....

Recipe Nº. 104 ....

Recipe Nº. 105 ....

Recipe Nº. 106 ....

Recipe Nº. 107 ....

Recipe Nº. 108 ....

Recipe Nº. 109 ....

Recipe Nº. 110 ....

Recipe Nº. 111 ....

Recipe Nº. 112 ....

Recipe Nº. 113 ....

Recipe Nº. 114 ....

Recipe Nº. 115 ....

Recipe Nº. 116 ....

Recipe Nº. 117 ....

Recipe Nº. 118 ....

Recipe Nº. 119 ....

Recipe Nº. 120 ....

Recipe N°. 1:

....

Servings ....   **Prep time** ....   **Cook time** ....

Ingredients: ## Directions:

....
....
....
....
....
....
....
....
....
....
....
....
....
....
....
....
....

Notes:

....
....
....
....
....
....
....
....

Recise N°. 2:

....

Servings   Prep time   Cook time

Ingredients: **Directions:**

....

....

....

....

....

....

....

....

....

....

....

....

....

....

....

....

....

 Notes:

....

....

....

....

....

....

....

....

Recipe N°. 3:

....

🍴 .... 🔧 .... } ....
Servings　　　　　Prep time　　　　Cook time

📋 Ingredients:　　📋 Directions:

....
....
....
....
....
....
....
....
....
....
....
....
....
....
....
....
....

 Notes:

....
....
....
....
....
....
....
....

Recipe N°. 4:

🍴 .... Servings   🛠 .... Prep time   } .... Cook time

📋 Ingredients: 📋 Directions:

📝 Notes:

Recipe Nº. 5:

....

🍴 ·················
Servings

🔧 ·················
Prep time

} ·················
Cook time

📋 Ingredients:

☑ Directions:

 Notes:

Recipe Nº. 6:

....

🍴 .... Servings   🛠 .... Prep time   } .... Cook time

📋 Ingredients: 📋 Directions:

....

....

....

....

....

....

....

....

....

....

....

....

....

....

....

....

....

....

 Notes:

....

....

....

....

....

....

....

....

Recipe Nº. 7: ....

🍴 .... Servings   🛠 .... Prep time   } .... Cook time

📋 Ingredients: ☑ Directions:

 Notes:

Recycle Nº. 8: ....

🍴 .... Servings   ⚒ .... Prep time   } .... Cook time

📋 Ingredients: 📋 Directions:

.... | ....

.... | ....

.... | ....

.... | ....

.... | ....

.... | ....

.... | ....

.... | ....

.... | ....

.... | ....

.... | ....

.... | ....

.... | ....

.... | ....

.... | ....

.... | ....

.... | ....

 Notes:

....

....

....

....

....

....

....

Recipe N°. 9:

....

🍴 ....   Servings   ⚒ ....   Prep time   } ....   Cook time

📋 Ingredients: 📝 Directions:

 Notes:

....
....
....
....
....
....
....

Recipe N⁰. 10:

🍴 .... Servings   ✖ .... Prep time   } .... Cook time

📋 Ingredients: 📋 Directions:

 Notes:

Recipe Nº. 11: ....

🍴 .... Servings   ⚒ .... Prep time   } .... Cook time

📋 Ingredients: 📋 Directions:

....
....
....
....
....
....
....
....
....
....
....
....
....
....
....
....
....
....

 Notes:

....
....
....
....
....
....
....
....

Recipe Nº. 12:

 Servings   Prep time   } Cook time

 Ingredients: Directions:

 Notes:

Recipe Nº. 13:

🍴 .... Servings   ⚒ .... Prep time   } .... Cook time

📋 Ingredients: 📋 Directions:

 Notes:

Recipe N°. 14: ....

Servings

Prep time

Cook time

 Ingredients:

Directions:

....
....
....
....
....
....
....
....
....
....
....
....
....
....
....
....
....
....

Notes:

Recipe Nº. 15:

🍴 .... Servings   🛠 .... Prep time   } .... Cook time

📋 Ingredients: ☑ Directions:

 Notes:

Recice Nº. 16: ....

🍴 .... Servings   ⚒ .... Prep time   } .... Cook time

📋 Ingredients: 📋 Directions:

📝 Notes:

Recipe N°. 17:

🍴 .... Servings   ⚒ .... Prep time   } .... Cook time

📋 Ingredients: ☑ Directions:

 Notes:

Recipe Nº. 18: ....

🍴 .... ✂ .... } ....
   Servings   Prep time   Cook time

📋 Ingredients: 📋 Directions:

 Notes:

....
....
....
....
....
....
....
....

Recipe Nº. 19:

....

🍴 .... **Servings**   ⚒ .... **Prep time**   } .... **Cook time**

📋 **Ingredients:**   📋 **Directions:**

 Notes:

Recipe N⁰. 20:

🍴 Servings   🛠 Prep time   } Cook time

📋 Ingredients: 📋 Directions:

 Notes:

Recipe N°. 21:

....

🍴 .... **Servings**　　　🛠 .... **Prep time**　　　} .... **Cook time**

📋 Ingredients:　　　🗒 Directions:

....　|　..
....　|　..
....　|　..
....　|　..
....　|　..
....　|　..
....　|　..
....　|　..
....　|　..
....　|　..
....　|　..
....　|　..
....　|　..
....　|　..
....　|　..
....　|　..
....　|　..

 Notes:

....
....
....
....
....
....
....
....

Recipe Nº. 22: ....

🍴 ....
Servings

🛠 ....
Prep time

} ....
Cook time

📋 Ingredients:

☑ Directions:

....
....
....
....
....
....
....
....
....
....
....
....
....
....
....
....
....

 Notes:

....
....
....
....
....
....
....
....

Recipe Nº. 23:

....

🍴 .... 🔧 .... } ....
   Servings   Prep time   Cook time

📋 Ingredients: 📋 Directions:

 Notes:

....

Recipe N°. 24: ....

🍴 ....   ✗ ....   } ....
Servings   Prep time   Cook time

📋 Ingredients: 📋 Directions:

 Notes:

....
....
....
....
....
....
....
....

Recipe Nº. 25:

🍴 .... Servings   🔧 .... Prep time   } .... Cook time

📋 Ingredients:

📋 Directions:

 Notes:

Recipe N°. 26: ....

🍴 .... Servings   ⚒ .... Prep time   } .... Cook time

📋 Ingredients: 📋 Directions:

....

....

....

....

....

....

....

....

....

....

....

....

....

....

....

....

....

 Notes:

....

....

....

....

....

....

....

....

Recipe N°. 27:

Servings ....   **Prep time** ....   **Cook time** ....

Ingredients:

Directions:

 Notes:

Recipe Nº. 28:

🍴 Servings   ⚒ Prep time   } Cook time

📋 Ingredients: 📋 Directions:

 Notes:

Recipe N°. 29:

🍴 .... Servings 🔧 .... Prep time } .... Cook time

📋 Ingredients: 📋 Directions:

 Notes:

Recipe N⁰. 30: ....

🍴 .... Servings   ✂ .... Prep time   } .... Cook time

📋 Ingredients: 📋 Directions:

....
....
....
....
....
....
....
....
....
....
....
....
....
....
....
....
....
....

 Notes:

....
....
....
....
....
....
....
....

Recipe Nº. 31:

....

🍴 .... **Servings**

🛠 .... **Prep time**

} .... **Cook time**

📋 **Ingredients:**   🗒 **Directions:**

....	....
....	....
....	....
....	....
....	....
....	....
....	....
....	....
....	....
....	....
....	....
....	....
....	....
....	....
....	....
....	....
....	....

 Notes:

....

....

....

....

....

....

....

Recipe Nº. 32: ....

🍴 .... Servings   🛠 .... Prep time   } .... Cook time

📋 Ingredients: 📋 Directions:

.... | ....
.... | ....
.... | ....
.... | ....
.... | ....
.... | ....
.... | ....
.... | ....
.... | ....
.... | ....
.... | ....
.... | ....
.... | ....
.... | ....
.... | ....
.... | ....
.... | ....
.... | ....

 Notes:

....
....
....
....
....
....
....
....

Recipe N°. 33:

....

🍴 .... Servings

⚒ .... Prep time

} .... Cook time

📋 Ingredients: ☑ Directions:

📝 Notes:

....
....
....
....
....
....
....
....

Recipe N⁰. 34: ....

Servings ....   Prep time ....   Cook time ....

Ingredients: **Directions:**

.... | ....
.... | ....
.... | ....
.... | ....
.... | ....
.... | ....
.... | ....
.... | ....
.... | ....
.... | ....
.... | ....
.... | ....
.... | ....
.... | ....
.... | ....
.... | ....
.... | ....

 Notes:

....
....
....
....
....
....
....
....

Recipe N°. 35:

....

🍴 .... Servings   🛠 .... Prep time   } .... Cook time

📋 Ingredients: ☑ Directions:

 Notes:

....
....
....
....
....
....
....
....

Recipe N°. 36:

🍴 .... Servings 🛠 .... Prep time } .... Cook time

📋 Ingredients: 📋 Directions:

📝 Notes:

Recipe N°. 37:

....

🍴 .... Servings
🔧 .... Prep time
} .... Cook time

📋 Ingredients:

📋 Directions:

....
....
....
....
....
....
....
....
....
....
....
....
....
....
....
....
....
....

 Notes:

....
....
....
....
....
....
....
....

Recipe N°. 38:

🍴 .... Servings   ⚒ .... Prep time   } .... Cook time

📋 Ingredients: ☑ Directions:

📝 Notes:

Recipe N°. 39:

Servings ....

Prep time ....

Cook time ....

Ingredients:

Directions:

 Notes:

Recipe N⁰. 40:

🍴 Servings   ⚒ Prep time   } Cook time

📋 Ingredients: 📋 Directions:

 Notes:

Recipe N°. 41:

🍴 .... Servings 🔧 .... Prep time } .... Cook time

📋 Ingredients: ☑️ Directions:

 Notes:

Recipe N°. 42: ....

🍴 ....
Servings

🔧 ....
Prep time

} ....
Cook time

📋 Ingredients: 📋 Directions:

.... | ....
.... | ....
.... | ....
.... | ....
.... | ....
.... | ....
.... | ....
.... | ....
.... | ....
.... | ....
.... | ....
.... | ....
.... | ....
.... | ....
.... | ....
.... | ....
.... | ....

 Notes:

....
....
....
....
....
....
....
....

Recipe Nº. 43:

....

🍴 .... Servings   ⚒ .... Prep time   } .... Cook time

📋 Ingredients: 📋 Directions:

 Notes:

Recipe Nº. 44:

🍴 Servings   ⚒ Prep time   } Cook time

📋 Ingredients:

📋 Directions:

 Notes:

Recipe N°. 45:

....

🍴 .... Servings   ⚒ .... Prep time   } .... Cook time

📋 Ingredients: ☑ Directions:

.... | ....

.... | ....

.... | ....

.... | ....

.... | ....

.... | ....

.... | ....

.... | ....

.... | ....

.... | ....

.... | ....

.... | ....

.... | ....

.... | ....

.... | ....

.... | ....

 Notes:

....

....

....

....

....

....

....

Recipe N°. 46:

🍴 Servings   ⚒ Prep time   } Cook time

📋 Ingredients: 📋 Directions:

 Notes:

Recipe N⁰. 47:

....

🍴 .... Servings

🔧 .... Prep time

} .... Cook time

📋 Ingredients:

📋 Directions:

.... | ....
.... | ....
.... | ....
.... | ....
.... | ....
.... | ....
.... | ....
.... | ....
.... | ....
.... | ....
.... | ....
.... | ....
.... | ....
.... | ....
.... | ....
.... | ....
.... | ....

 Notes:

....
....
....
....
....
....
....
....

Recipe Nº. 48:

🍴 .... Servings   ⚒ .... Prep time   } .... Cook time

📋 Ingredients: 📋 Directions:

 Notes:

Recipe Nº. 49:

Servings .... **Prep time** .... **Cook time** ....

Ingredients:

Directions:

 Notes:

Recipe Nº. 50:

....

🍴 .... Servings   🛠 .... Prep time   } .... Cook time

📋 Ingredients: 📋 Directions:

 Notes:

Recipe N°. 51:

....

🍴 ....
Servings

🛠 ....
Prep time

} ....
Cook time

📋 Ingredients:

📋 Directions:

....
....
....
....
....
....
....
....
....
....
....
....
....
....
....
....
....

 Notes:

....
....
....
....
....
....
....
....

Recipe Nº. 52: ....

🍴 .... Servings   🛠 .... Prep time   } .... Cook time

📋 Ingredients: 📋 Directions:

.... | ....
.... | ....
.... | ....
.... | ....
.... | ....
.... | ....
.... | ....
.... | ....
.... | ....
.... | ....
.... | ....
.... | ....
.... | ....
.... | ....
.... | ....
.... | ....
.... | ....
.... | ....

 Notes:

....
....
....
....
....
....
....
....

52

Recipe N°. 53:

....

🍴 .... Servings   ⚒ .... Prep time   } .... Cook time

📋 Ingredients: ☑ Directions:

....
....
....
....
....
....
....
....
....
....
....
....
....
....
....
....
....

 Notes:

....
....
....
....
....
....
....
....

Recipe Nº. 54:

....

🍴 .... Servings   ⚒ .... Prep time   } .... Cook time

📋 Ingredients: 📋 Directions:

....
....
....
....
....
....
....
....
....
....
....
....
....
....
....
....
....

 Notes:

....
....
....
....
....
....
....
....

Recipe Nº. 55:

....

🍴 .... Servings ⚒ .... Prep time } .... Cook time

📋 Ingredients:

📋 Directions:

 Notes:

Recipe Nº. 56:

🍴 Servings   ⚒ Prep time   } Cook time

📋 Ingredients: 📋 Directions:

 Notes:

Recipe Nº. 57:

....

🍴 .... Servings

🔧 .... Prep time

} .... Cook time

📋 Ingredients:

📝 Directions:

....
....
....
....
....
....
....
....
....
....
....
....
....
....
....
....
....

 Notes:

....
....
....
....
....
....
....
....

Recipe N°. 58:

....

🍴 .... **Servings**   🔧 .... **Prep time**   } .... **Cook time**

📋 Ingredients: 📋 Directions:

....
....
....
....
....
....
....
....
....
....
....
....
....
....
....
....
....
....

 Notes:

....
....
....
....
....
....
....
....

Recipe Nº. 59:

....

🍴 .... Servings

🔧 .... Prep time

} .... Cook time

📋 Ingredients:

☑️ Directions:

Ingredients	Directions
....	....
....	....
....	....
....	....
....	....
....	....
....	....
....	....
....	....
....	....
....	....
....	....
....	....
....	....
....	....
....	....
....	....
....	....

📝 Notes:

....
....
....
....
....
....
....
....

Recipe Nº. 60: ....

🍴 .... Servings ⚒ .... Prep time } .... Cook time

📋 Ingredients: 📋 Directions:

....
....
....
....
....
....
....
....
....
....
....
....
....
....
....
....
....
....

 Notes:

....
....
....
....
....
....
....
....

Recipe N°. 61:

....

🍴 .... Servings   🔧 .... Prep time   } .... Cook time

📋 Ingredients: ✅ Directions:

 Notes:

....
....
....
....
....
....
....
....

Recipe Nº. 62: ....

🍴 .... 🔧 .... } ....
Servings Prep time Cook time

📋 Ingredients: 📋 Directions:

....
....
....
....
....
....
....
....
....
....
....
....
....
....
....
....
....
....
....

 Notes:

....
....
....
....
....
....
....
....

Recide Nº. 63:

🍴 Servings   🔧 Prep time   } Cook time

📋 Ingredients:

☑ Directions:

 Notes:

Recipe N⁰. 64:

Servings .... **Prep time** .... **Cook time** ....

Ingredients:

Directions:

Notes:

Recipe Nº. 65:

🍴 Servings   ✂️ Prep time   } Cook time

📋 Ingredients: 🗒 Directions:

 Notes:

Recipe Nº. 66:

....

🍴 ....
Servings

🔧 ....
Prep time

} ....
Cook time

📋 Ingredients:

📋 Directions:

....
....
....
....
....
....
....
....
....
....
....
....
....
....
....
....
....

📝 Notes:

....
....
....
....
....
....
....
....

Recipe Nº. 67:

🍴 .... Servings 🔧 .... Prep time } .... Cook time

📋 Ingredients: ☑ Directions:

....

 Notes:

Recipe Nº. 68:

....

🍴 .... Servings

🔧 .... Prep time

} .... Cook time

📋 Ingredients:

📋 Directions:

....

....

....

....

....

....

....

....

....

....

....

....

....

....

....

....

....

....

📝 Notes:

....

....

....

....

....

....

....

Recipe Nº. 69:

🍴 .... Servings   ✂️ .... Prep time   } .... Cook time

📋 Ingredients: ☑️ Directions:

 Notes:

Recipe Nº. 70:

....

🍴 .... **Servings**   🛠 .... **Prep time**   } .... **Cook time**

📋 **Ingredients:**   📋 **Directions:**

.... | ....
.... | ....
.... | ....
.... | ....
.... | ....
.... | ....
.... | ....
.... | ....
.... | ....
.... | ....
.... | ....
.... | ....
.... | ....
.... | ....
.... | ....
.... | ....
.... | ....

 Notes:

....
....
....
....
....
....
....

Recipe N°. 71:

....

🍴 .... Servings   🔧 .... Prep time   } .... Cook time

📋 Ingredients: 📋 Directions:

 Notes:

....
....
....
....
....
....
....
....

Recipe Nº. 72: ....

🍴 ....   Servings   ✂ .... Prep time   } .... Cook time

📋 Ingredients: 📋 Directions:

....
....
....
....
....
....
....
....
....
....
....
....
....
....
....
....
....
....

 Notes:

....
....
....
....
....
....
....
....

Recipe Nº. 73: ....

🍴 .... Servings   🔧 .... Prep time   } .... Cook time

📋 Ingredients: 📋 Directions:

Notes:

Recipe Nº. 74:

🍴 ....
Servings

🛠 ....
Prep time

} ....
Cook time

📋 Ingredients:

📋 Directions:

 Notes:

Recipe N°. 75:

 Servings   Prep time   Cook time

Ingredients: Directions:

 Notes:

Recipe Nº. 76:

🍴 .... Servings   ⚒ .... Prep time   } .... Cook time

📋 Ingredients: ☑ Directions:

 Notes:

Recipe Nº. 77: ....

🍴 .... Servings   ✂️ .... Prep time   } .... Cook time

📋 Ingredients: 📋 Directions:

.... | ....
.... | ....
.... | ....
.... | ....
.... | ....
.... | ....
.... | ....
.... | ....
.... | ....
.... | ....
.... | ....
.... | ....
.... | ....
.... | ....
.... | ....
.... | ....
.... | ....
.... | ....

 Notes:

....
....
....
....
....
....
....

Recipe N°. 78: ....

🍴 .... Servings   🛠 .... Prep time   } .... Cook time

📋 Ingredients: 📋 Directions:

.... | ....
.... | ....
.... | ....
.... | ....
.... | ....
.... | ....
.... | ....
.... | ....
.... | ....
.... | ....
.... | ....
.... | ....
.... | ....
.... | ....
.... | ....
.... | ....
.... | ....
.... | ....

 Notes:

....
....
....
....
....
....
....

Recipe Nº. 79:

🍴 .... Servings ⚒ .... Prep time } .... Cook time

📋 Ingredients:　　📋 Directions:

 Notes:

Recipe N⁰. 80:

🍴 Servings   ⚒ Prep time   } Cook time

📋 Ingredients: ☑ Directions:

 Notes:

Recipe Nº. 81: ....

🍴 .... Servings   🔧 .... Prep time   } .... Cook time

📋 Ingredients: 🗒 Directions:

 Notes:

Recipe Nº. 82: ....

🍴 .... Servings   ✂️ .... Prep time   } .... Cook time

📋 Ingredients: ☑️ Directions:

....
....
....
....
....
....
....
....
....
....
....
....
....
....
....
....
....
....

 Notes:

....
....
....
....
....
....
....
....

Recipe N°. 83: ....

🍴 .... Servings   🛠 .... Prep time   } .... Cook time

📋 Ingredients: 📋 Directions:

.... | ....
.... | ....
.... | ....
.... | ....
.... | ....
.... | ....
.... | ....
.... | ....
.... | ....
.... | ....
.... | ....
.... | ....
.... | ....
.... | ....
.... | ....
.... | ....
.... | ....
.... | ....

 Notes:

....
....
....
....
....
....
....
....

Recipe N°. 84:

....

🍴 .... **Servings**   ⚒ .... **Prep time**   } .... **Cook time**

📋 Ingredients: 📋 Directions:

....

📝 Notes:

....

Recipe N°. 85:

....

🍴 .... Servings   🛠 .... Prep time   } .... Cook time

📋 Ingredients: 📋 Directions:

 Notes:

Recipe Nº. 86:

🍴 .... Servings   ⚒ .... Prep time   } .... Cook time

📋 Ingredients: 📋 Directions:

Notes:

Recipe N⁰. 87:

....

🍴 .... Servings   🛠 .... Prep time   } .... Cook time

📋 Ingredients: 🗒 Directions:

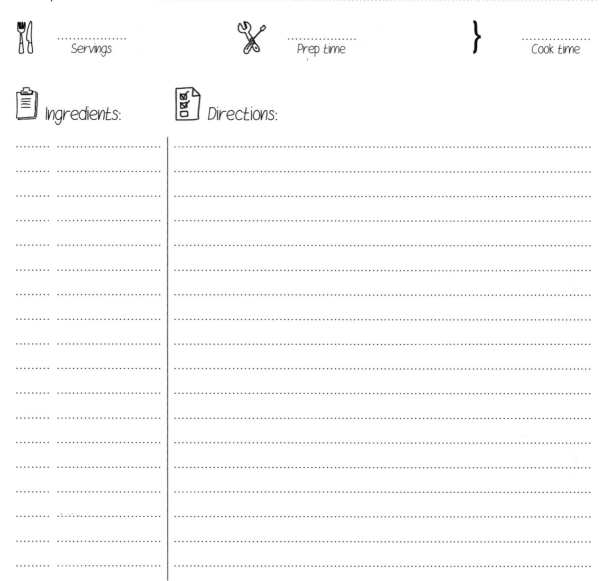

📝 Notes:

....
....
....
....
....
....
....
....

Recipe Nº. 88:

....

🍴 .... Servings   ⚒ .... Prep time   } .... Cook time

📋 Ingredients: 📋 Directions:

 Notes:

Recipe Nº. 89:

🍴 Servings ⚒ Prep time ⎰ Cook time

📋 Ingredients: ☑ Directions:

 Notes:

Recipe N°. 90:

....

🍴 .... Servings   ⚒ .... Prep time   } .... Cook time

📋 Ingredients: 📋 Directions:

 Notes:

....

....

....

....

....

....

....

....

Recipe Nº. 91:

🍴 .... Servings   ✂ .... Prep time   } .... Cook time

📋 Ingredients: 📋 Directions:

....
....
....
....
....
....
....
....
....
....
....
....
....
....
....
....
....
....

 Notes:

....
....
....
....
....
....
....

Recive N°. 92: ....

🍴 .... Servings   ✂ .... Prep time   } .... Cook time

📋 Ingredients: ☑ Directions:

.... | ....
.... | ....
.... | ....
.... | ....
.... | ....
.... | ....
.... | ....
.... | ....
.... | ....
.... | ....
.... | ....
.... | ....
.... | ....
.... | ....
.... | ....
.... | ....
.... | ....

 Notes:

....
....
....
....
....
....
....
....

Recipe Nº. 93:

🍴 Servings   ✂ Prep time   } Cook time

📋 Ingredients: ☑ Directions:

 Notes:

Recipe N⁰. 94: ....

🍴 .... ⚒ .... } ....
　Servings 　　　　　 Prep time 　　　　　 Cook time

📋 Ingredients:　　📋 Directions:

....
....
....
....
....
....
....
....
....
....
....
....
....
....
....
....
....
....

 Notes:

....
....
....
....
....
....
....
....

Recipe Nº. 95: ....

🍴 .... Servings   🛠 .... Prep time   } .... Cook time

📋 Ingredients: 📝 Directions:

 Notes:

Recipe N°. 96:

 Servings

 Prep time

} Cook time

 Ingredients:

Directions:

 Notes:

Recipe Nº. 97:

🍴 .... Servings   🛠 .... Prep time   } .... Cook time

📋 Ingredients: 📋 Directions:

 Notes:

Recipe Nº. 98:

....

🍴 .... Servings   ✂️ .... Prep time   } .... Cook time

📋 Ingredients:

☑️ Directions:

....

....

....

....

....

....

....

....

....

....

....

....

....

....

....

....

....

....

 Notes:

....

....

....

....

....

....

....

....

Recipe Nº. 99:

....

🍴 .... Servings   ✂ .... Prep time   } .... Cook time

📋 Ingredients: ☑ Directions:

 Notes:

Recice Nº. 100: ....

 Servings ....   Prep time ....   } Cook time ....

 Ingredients: Directions:

Notes:

Recipe Nº. 101:

🍴 Servings   🔧 Prep time   } Cook time

📋 Ingredients: 📝 Directions:

 Notes:

Recipe N⁰. 102:

 Servings   Prep time   } Cook time

 Ingredients: Directions:

 Notes:

Recipe Nº. 103:

🍴 Servings   ⚒ Prep time   } Cook time

📋 Ingredients: 📋 Directions:

.... | ....
.... | ....
.... | ....
.... | ....
.... | ....
.... | ....
.... | ....
.... | ....
.... | ....
.... | ....
.... | ....
.... | ....
.... | ....
.... | ....
.... | ....
.... | ....
.... | ....
.... | ....

 Notes:

....
....
....
....
....
....
....
....

Recipe N°. 104: ....

  Servings   Prep time   } Cook time

Ingredients: Directions:

 Notes:

Recipe Nº. 105: ....

🍴 Servings ....   ✂ Prep time ....   } Cook time ....

📋 Ingredients: 📋 Directions:

.... | ....
.... | ....
.... | ....
.... | ....
.... | ....
.... | ....
.... | ....
.... | ....
.... | ....
.... | ....
.... | ....
.... | ....
.... | ....
.... | ....
.... | ....
.... | ....
.... | ....

 Notes:

....
....
....
....
....
....
....
....

Recipe Nº. 106:

  Servings

 Prep time

} Cook time

 Ingredients:

Directions:

 Notes:

Recipe N°. 107:

....

🍴 .... Servings   🔧 .... Prep time   } .... Cook time

📋 Ingredients: 📋 Directions:

 Notes:

....
....
....
....
....
....
....
....

Recipe N°. 108: ....

🍴 .... **Servings** ⚒ .... **Prep time** } .... **Cook time**

📋 Ingredients: ☑ Directions:

....

....

....

....

....

....

....

....

....

....

....

....

....

....

....

....

....

 Notes:

....

....

....

....

....

....

....

Recipe N°. 109:

🍴 Servings   🔧 Prep time   } Cook time

📋 Ingredients: 📋 Directions:

 Notes:

Recipe Nº. 110:

....

🍴 .... 🛠 .... } ....
Servings Prep time Cook time

📋 Ingredients: 📋 Directions:

....
....
....
....
....
....
....
....
....
....
....
....
....
....
....
....
....

 Notes:

....
....
....
....
....
....
....

Recipe N°. 111:

....

🍴 .... Servings   🔧 .... Prep time   } .... Cook time

📋 Ingredients: 📋 Directions:

.... | ....
.... | ....
.... | ....
.... | ....
.... | ....
.... | ....
.... | ....
.... | ....
.... | ....
.... | ....
.... | ....
.... | ....
.... | ....
.... | ....
.... | ....
.... | ....
.... | ....

 Notes:

....
....
....
....
....
....
....
....

Recipe N⁰. 112:

....

🍴 .... Servings

✂️ .... Prep time

} .... Cook time

📋 Ingredients:

📋 Directions:

....
....
....
....
....
....
....
....
....
....
....
....
....
....
....
....

 Notes:

....
....
....
....
....
....
....

Recipe Nº. 113:

 Servings   Prep time   } Cook time

 Ingredients: Directions:

 Notes:

Recipe N°. 114:

Servings   Prep time   Cook time

Ingredients: **Directions:**

 Notes:

Recipe Nº. 115:

🍴 Servings   ✂️ Prep time   } Cook time

📋 Ingredients: 📋 Directions:

 Notes:

Recipe N°. 116:

....

🍴 .... Servings   🛠 .... Prep time   } .... Cook time

📋 Ingredients: 📋 Directions:

Ingredients	Directions
....	....
....	....
....	....
....	....
....	....
....	....
....	....
....	....
....	....
....	....
....	....
....	....
....	....
....	....
....	....
....	....

 Notes:

....
....
....
....
....
....
....
....

Recipe N°. 117:

....

🍴 .... Servings   ✂️ .... Prep time   } .... Cook time

📋 Ingredients: 📋 Directions:

 Notes:

....
....
....
....
....
....
....

Recipe N°. 118: ....

🍴 ....   ⚒ ....   } ....
Servings   Prep time   Cook time

📋 Ingredients: 📋 Directions:

 Notes:

Recipe N°. 119:

🍴 .... Servings   🔧 .... Prep time   } .... Cook time

📋 Ingredients: 📋 Directions:

 Notes:

Recipe N⁰. 120: ....

 .... Servings   .... Prep time   } .... Cook time

 Ingredients: Directions:

....
....
....
....
....
....
....
....
....
....
....
....
....
....
....
....
....

 Notes:

....
....
....
....
....
....
....
....

 Notes